melancholy of a mystique medley dream ..

& other selected poetry

prasad hirsch

melancholy of a mystique medley dream .. & other selected poetry

to my girlfriend ..

...

the trees all around reinstates them

with happiness and fervour,

reassures and inspires them with

the splendid song of its zeal,

the little bit of shade every last one of them render,

is quite a synonym of love ...

the song of magnolia..

table of contents

1
kissing the mist on his whisky glass ..

kissing the mist on his whisky glass ..

while in those deep dark woods of the early dawn's gloom

amidst a dense fog and chill air,
you are lying beside the burnt down ashes,

the smoke coming out of last night's fire

around those dry leaves and dark mud beneath the huge barks,

hardly you could open your eyes the lids so tight and drowsy
deprived of sleep the stoned you,

could 'nt get up out of weary

and whole night of scripting alongside your cognac,
your eyes could barely open nor see anything around

though you still try and half opened lids could see

the sort of trees tilted, your black ash tray with a few white
buds,

ashes and specks oozing out the last bit of smoke,

you could see your lady dancing in curves eluding you in the
deep woods,

1instigated by the emanating edge's curvy waves

to a slender long arc of his lady's moves

so exquisite and so delusional goes her ways oozing and swinging,

kissing the mist over his whisky glass in the prevailing hazy gloom.

2
the magical lambent light
of virgin moon

the magical lambent light of virgin moon ..

its a starry night with the lovely white gleam

and such beautiful glades of the white lucency

that is dipping the night in a scintillating mood

of lute and romance.

the ride over the country side highway

while playing the sinatra's jazz

as it goes like ' fly me to the moon,

let me play among the stars ... ',

swings up the mates to a ethereal very moon glide.

a lovely girl of eighteen with long curly hairs

looking petite and pale,

is all excited and brimming perhaps

in their first date.

with a sexy exposing black top

and a short skirt, revealing her skin's lustre,

that would turn her mate on and wild,

she has removed her jacket off,

trying to imitate her cozy neighbour

drawn by her ways and attitude.

driving his dad's car, the cool dude

is so sturdy and macho in a sleeve less tee and shorts,

as if like a pro in stalking.

her charm and his charisma,

alluring to each other just as their mood,

magic and the moonlight.

they are riding along on a weekend getaway,

in this long straight highway

amidst the prevailing magic, music

and the moonlit refulgence.

the almost desolated road with none else

in the drive along this stretch taking them

beside en route a lovely song of lavender,

raising the scent around the glistening air

of countless silver scintillas,

that oozes out the fulgere of such enthralling romance,

that gushes out the music and song

behind the scene's glitz and glam.

the gleaming moonlight through the window

glistens her face with the white

and sheen of the moon river,

that streaming down rays descending

into their space in subtle lambency

and in sensual flow of lustre and love,

gliding them up onto a milder arousal flight

to the lusty moon river of scintillas and sparkles

and they shine in diamond sheen each and every one of them,

those miniature lozenges of the moon fragment,

those tiny crescents of scintillating chemistry,

and the minuscule starry specks

of love libidos, the glitzy daze,

of such sizzling romance

and the hayday gay of young inside's merriment

over their first date make out,

as they smooch and cuddle lovingly

under the shinning silverlight glittering

in enchanted blithe mirrored by those refulgent eyes,

as they intertwine fondly revelling in the moonlight kiss,

while the gutsy lad with his kissing babe says ,

' love you to the moon and back... ',

under the magical lambent light

of the virgin moon's celestial beauty.

3
the song of magnolia ..

the song of magnolia ..

a unique huge pathway in that mammoth park,

with quite a number of people fluctuating by,

you could see lively young lovers strolling

with their hands clasped tight

just as their hearts in true love's bind,

while the girlie leaning on her boy's shoulder

feeling his warmth and brace,

a group of young dudes moving swiftly

around half a dozen yards behind these cute lovers,

they seem to imitate the kind of beatles' fashion,

wherein wrapped in skinny denims and tee

and almost alike band of dudes with one in long hair

of a dirty rapper and an other in wayfarer,

one more in bleached head with a guitar in his back,

they seem to be quietly roving on in a milder muse

preoccupied in something, perhaps over

their intriguing session of lyrical annotations

from the likes of Dylan's and Hendrix's

to enhance their versing flow.

a couple of old gentlemen

walking adjacent to them in the other side,

in their joggers' attire posing quite a prim

demeanour and a primp grooming,

stiffly moving ahead chatting about dogmatically

on locale politics may be, certainly seems like

trying to rationale their views

in quick strides along the lane,

few children running around and playing

inside the lane tossing the balls and pebbles,

while a little boy is curiously probing

the dark brown ridged bark in the lane's side

as he tries to hug it and lean over it

perhaps with a sense of nonchalant empathy over its stand,

while another of them a lovely cute girl

in beautiful pink frock is looking

to pluck a flower as equally roseate in a juxtapose,

admiring the beauty of the morning bloom's

petals and the stupendous colours of such

cherishing joy and flourishing bliss amongst

the nature's awe inspiring magnolia.

the oaks and pines that stands tall inside this beautiful park ,

renders the serene radiance of solace and light,

the rays that would gleam folks with the soothing aura

for those in bitterness and harsh days

lacking the ambien's quenching comfort

for the diverged you,

without the place's quaint lull of divulging serenity

for the depressed you,

the slow rendition of the calming melancholy

that this vast gardenia tries to paint

inside the minds of the dwelling folks,

would certainly lift you up

and console you with respite,

the seats of leisure inside rests them

with kindness and regroups them

lifting their spirits high,

exhilarating them with the poise of the pleasant gardenia,

the floral blooms and lush greens of the arena

instigate people with love and light,

converging them with angelic sheen,

invigorating joy and the bliss of magnolia.

the inspiring blossoms and colours of the scenic around

instills folks with lustre and inculcates them

with the luminance and persistence of a decades old art,

the indistinct medley of its sanguine beauty

and the nuances behind,

illuminating them with congruence

of ardour, amour and delight.

the trees all around reinstates them

with happiness and fervour,

reassures and inspires them with

the splendid song of its zeal,

the little bit of shade every last one of them render,

is quite a synonym of love.

4
palattes of paint, mirth & brace

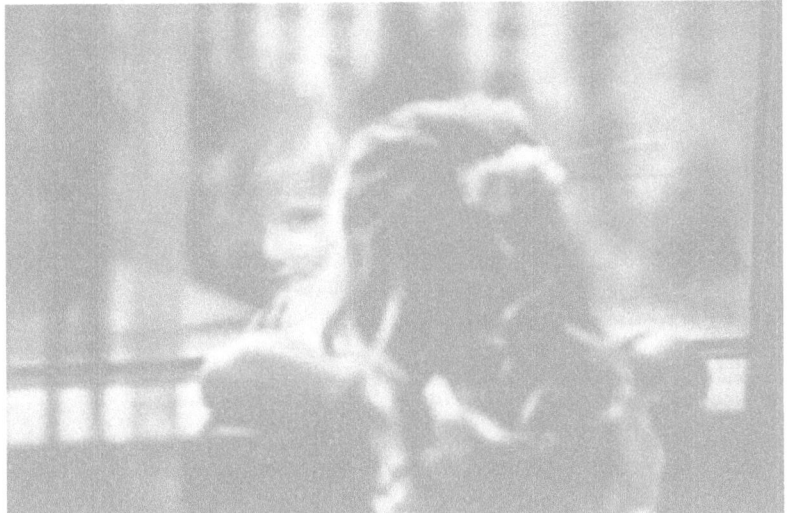

palattes of paint, mirth and brace ..

he is all bored and dull,

lacking her usual josh,

perhaps her early days at school

is making her feel uncomfortable,

with the air of unease surrounding her

all the while inside this new place of hers,

not able to fit in with the folks around,

drooping down sluggishly inactive,

keeping calm and mum feeling so gloomy,

seems a bit queer cute little girlie,

keeping herself quite aloof from the surrounding,

her inchoate mind is not able to read

the scenario's entailed discipline,

wherein she seems to move herself out from the bunch,

lacking that thing inside her

to accept the scene around,

to accept her kinder folks around

sans that gel that every other kid has,

she is all slumber and bit sloppy

hardly with any vague idea

why she isn't feeling the same way

as she would do at home,

while her slothful and unparticipative mood

with her class makes her seem floppy and low,

her lazy legs and passive mind is

apparently gesturing her teacher

to care more for the kid,

to look after her in uncommon attention,

worrying her keeping her in a spot of bother.

and all the while the little girlie is

missing her home and thinking about

how happy and merry she would get around

unlike here at this dull and gloomy place

of hers turning her down in dismay.

she is all low, dull and seriously homesick

missing out on her mom,

missing out her care and warmth,

lacking her kissing embrace,

her love and her play,

her beautiful face,

her feel and her touch,

her affectionate words and her affable mirth,

the gay and hay, the joy and merry around,

her brother's play time,

the girlie's jollity out of the colors and

the toons in her tv while watching it alongside her mom,

missing out on her toys and blocks, her rings and dolls,

that she would love to play with,

the coloring pads and pens of such joy and delight

lighting her up, as she eagerly paints and scribbles

the exciting pages of merry,

with every stroke of the paint,

while in every streak of the scribble,

as she completes a sheet's colors,

she would be excited and glowing

in all her haven's love,

in all her sweet home's harmony,

the warmth and care behind,

the giggles and gay playing all around in sway,

the love and laughter enjoying around in glitter,

before the lovely angel dozes off

to sleep in comfort and care,

just when her mom puts down

her fairy tale read in kiss and flair.

She is dull and gloomy, lacking in lustre,

missing her home badly

standing before this window

leaning over it calm and quiet,

mum and in milder fright,

she looks out the window glass,

coy and timid she gazes out

through its transparent gloss,

the lush greens of the outside lawn

attracts her as she keeps her eyes

so fixed over its color,

its shades of the green and

the spread of playful joy,

reminding her of home's mirth and brace,

reminding her of the week before's

affable times of chromatic painting,

wherein she delightedly dipped her hands

in palattes of paints,

the affluent liquids of flourishing dreams,

pressing it hard over the sheet of joy and white,

as her mom helped her pressing

those lovable cute impressions

of this little angel's tiny soft hands,

those glittering imprints in flying colors,

tracing the shades of love and

the hues of trust and contours of glitz,

painting the impressioned colors

of a prolific rainbow,

the colors of harmony and bless.

She continues her gaze curiously

over the lawn and the people passing by,

and the parked cars, its colors and gloss,

leaning on that beautiful window wall,

attracted may be by its gleam and glide,

pulled by its sheen and reflection perhaps,

liking its feel of touch while sliding her fingers

over its smoothened surface's clarity of light,

unlike her rudimentary layer of observing knack,

thinking flow, conceiving ideas and cognitive learning,

as different from her little ignorant mind's

gloomy and hazy moods of insecure grey hues.

5
eternal flames of burning love

eternal flames of burning love ..

could sense such brightness of the eternal light,

so holy and serene they glow in undying passion,

the white of heaven should say.

Never have I seen a light so bright and so white,

burning like the heaven's fire of love,

the eternal flames of burning love.

Never have i seen such refulgent flames,

burning like the mammoth twinning strings of fire

intertwined in ardent passion and fervent amour,

so flawless and so pure,

the eternal flames of the burning love.

Perhaps should conceive it as a notion

to portray the intercourse the love

between the souls made for each other

through the conspiring universe's divine wish,

that tends to bring the mates together

wherever they are under sky.

Might even perceive it as a higher phenomenon

of the cosmic mythology

that symbolizes the prolonging conscious state

of togetherness between the souls

so as to attain the sort of a state

that strives to blend the mates united

and inseparable forever under sky.

Like the feathers of fire,

the eternal flames of burning love are sensually glowing,

twisted and twinning with each other,

with such profound enlightenment,

elucidating the forever consciousness

of the souls blended in higher desires.

Together the flames arise from the single ovoid

shinning in the light of eternal amour,

glowing in the inherent intricacies

of the universe's soul,

embodying the spirit of eternal flames

that tends to instill the intimate nexus,

the love symbol of divine wish,

the significant picture of the higher desires.

Never have i seen such flames of ethereal fulgere,

such immortal flames of the holy love

that might have taken its origin

from Greek gods and goddesses,

or could be the from the highness Aphrodite

or perhaps could even be from the very universe's soul,

the eternal flames of burning love.

6
the wreath of love ..

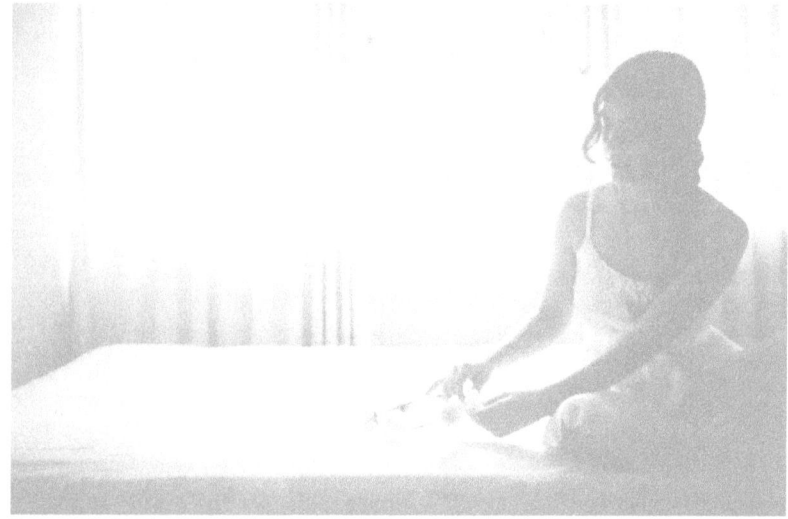

the wreath of love ..

its the kind of lazy afternoon gloom

you would end up with in some rare while.

she is inside this milder gloomy daze

today unlike her mundane.

The kind of a scintillating mood

While you dream about sizzling paris

When its lovers dance and romance, kiss and caress,

Under the grey skies in its brimming rainy evening

feeling the heavenly drizzle.

When you muse about your beau, love and all that jazz

brewing the wildest of dreams

brimming in with the girlie desires and passion

that burns so bright like sunshine,

that glows as in the flame of twine,

beneath the warmth and brace of the sensual fire,

alongside the love song of aphrodite

who wears the lovely myrtle's wreath

beautifying her inner effulgence and redolence,

and the highness her exquisite intimacy.

The charming girl of twenty two

looks gorgeous in her sexy white sleeve less attire.

Her dark black braid and the thin long necklace

the pedant that kisses her bosom underneath the white neckline,

makes you wonder is the very aphrodite in here,

perhaps the greek myth goddess has descended down

in a feminine incarnation with such exquisite beauty.

weaving in her dreams and desires

she does her wreath of lovely roses and lavender

singing her songs of passion and love,

she yearns for her days of roses and wine

she dances alone to her afternoon medley

grooving amidst the sizzling jazz

perhaps trying to migrate onto a wonderland salsa

in that gleaming ambien of sparkles and white

beside the white drapes and butterflies

flying around fluttering her wings

kissing the flowers woven in her wreath of love.

such a scintillating tango it is

blended in with her yearn and song,

the merry and hay,

the wine and roses,

the longing and love.

weaving in her dreams and desires

she does her wreath of lovely roses and lavender

perhaps she is writing her intimate letters

of love and passion heart inked

in deep felt romance, desires and longing.

ceaseless she seems to be in writing

though the count has crossed hundred and more

piling up her shelves.

as the beautiful flowers in wreath

blended in with her yearn and song,

the letters conveyed the girlie's man

her charm and splendour

the merry and hay,

the wine and roses,

the longing and love.

singing her songs of passion and love,

she dances alone to her afternoon medley

7
a daydream delusion ..

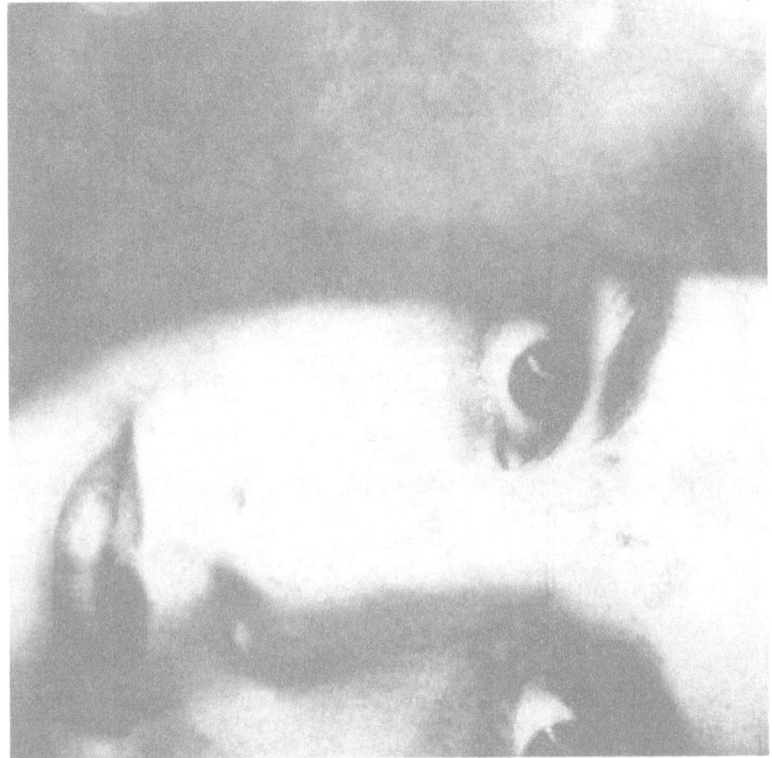

a daydream delusion ..

such thick black lovely brows stands beneath her beautiful dark eyes.

these are the eyes that tend to flight the spectre of love upon every man it sees.

The spectre of love that pulls anyone inside her hypnotic beauty, gathering one to her realm of charm and lure,

binding one into a infatuated gleamy continuum of enticing pulchritude,

which might seemingly tend to immerse him inside her gleaming gel of bait.

The diva's spectre might even arouse and mesmerize one alluring him to her enchanted aura.

Beside her window glasses with a cup of coffee and a book from danielle steel,

She seems to be on a muse looking through the window glass with the beautiful pouring silent rain.

The lovely daylight drizzle through the closed glass doors sans the sound of it.

Drawn in by the scintillating scene of the mood's medley and tired of her routine,

She seems to be on a muse looking at the sizzling rain outside, trying to converge her insides may be,

perhaps a trance they might call it sometimes.

May be she is trying to weave her threads of desires and passion

upon her delusional tapestry,

Should be playing inside her tunes of love,

that yodels inside her strings of longing and yearn

while painting her mind's awe,

its love and fervour,

the girlie desires and

the passion behind,

its mellifluous floral blooms

of the daydream magnolia,

shading its colors in undulating fragments

of lure and lustre,

hazily picturing inside her

woven tapestry of a lady's muse,

like a starry rain,

like a song of love,

inside her melancholic reverie.

She is immersed inside

in the soothing river of

a daydream delusion,

in the pleasasnt warmth

of a lady's muse and

in its underlying solitary melodrama,

floating inside her kissing reverie.

8
love is in the air ..

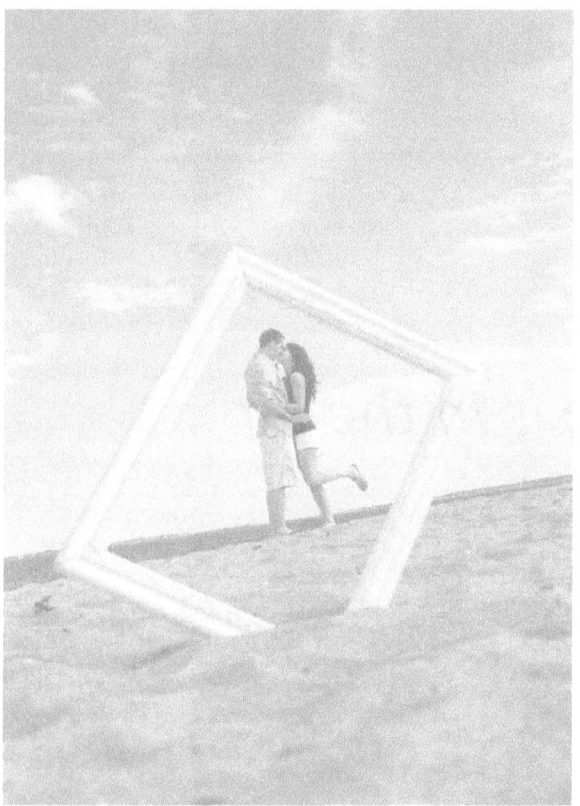

love is in the air ..

Well, a young couple out there in the sands of the beach

looking for the waving around free spirit of a wonderful hangout...

to feel the kiss of the early morning chill breeze

from the tidal waves for the exciting time around

in the almost deserted shore

over the cruising up moments of delicate nuances,

to smell the pleasant morning outset's air

 filled with the eternal love from the angels and cupids

that seems to fly around in a transparent attired outlay

over the colourful blue sky just like the shaping whiter clouds

with the flare of light and gloss tracing

their fountain of soaring up youth's intimacy,

glowing around the surrounding's beauty light

and love of heaven, for the fresh stroll of the day's dawn

while they muse and chat along on the long stride

of slow walk along the sea line

with ice cold waters kissing their toes,

for the play over the waves

romancing in the beach's ecstatic embrace

of the quiet and splendour breeze

while the lovers find themselves throwing waters,

kissing and smooching and even probably

for a mild intertwine laying out there in the none-else-found open,

to taste the pleasure of leisure time life on the essence

of a beach vacation over the uncared spirit

of lovely romantic chilling out sorts of exotic thrill,

to capture on a memory of a life time beautifully engraved

inside the white bounds of lasting romance

for the framed up everlasting kiss

thats gonna transcend feels of lovely nostalgia

and smiles of joy for the decades ahead

just like the elating delight

and sweet taste of the aging fine wine,

at a truly inner soul exhilarating

and a couple's bond refreshing spot of pure bliss

that limelights the hearts of love, that which soars up

the blended in romance deeply rooted inside,

just like the vastly expansed dark blue ocean

of scintillating dreams sizzling love and a beautiful life, the place that would make anyone there

to say "Love is in the air"!!!

9
a gloomy dusk's
cafe brew ..

While in those gloomy days of the early monsoon,

may be with a book of ayn rand or any other on metaphysics

and a mug of freshly brewed steamingly hot coffee,

you tend to keep yourself warm

inside your personal hub in your sweet home.

Perhaps like the brimming coffee in her hand,

she must be brewing her wilder dreams

of passion, love and all that jazz.

Seems like the evening petrichor is filling her ambience

with a air of nostalgia,

taking her down the lane

when she was enjoying that panorama

of beautiful scenic rainbow while in her grade four

after that sizzling drizzle of quieter evening

when she danced in the rain alongside her mom

playing with her as she felt the raising odour

of the wet sands and the raindrops

kissing her rosy cheeks drenching her all wet

while looking up at the sky's marvellous rainbow,

inspiring her colours and hues over the sizzling childhood

of a chromatic art sheet's thriving mirth,

picturing you the prolixity behind the period's growth

and accretion of individual's instigating inner elements

upon both physical and mental factors,

consequently the divulging ideas,

accumulated learning and the acquired sense,

premising the individual's curiosity, interests and knacks.

Seems like she is looking to gather her illuminated radiance

upon her ardent passion,

as when she tries to ray out her ways

in pursuing her agenda ahead,

hitting the road ahead,

while cruising the fervent road along,

that you wish to ride on,

you yearn to take amidst the congruence

of your culminated ideas,

environmental fostering and focused taming,

with that precise acumen and acquired potential

of eloquent knack and glowing flair.

Rejuvenating herself with the time's gloomy tone and jollity tint,

she must have been musing

about her agenda, road, life and all that jazz,

while basking in the feeling of the stance's limelight.

Also she must be all into her lovey-dovey

mood i presume, trying to picture

the glossy times with her beau

of a handsome hunk's demeanour,

may be craving for their candle-lit

datenight dinner's dessert scoop,

should be trying to dream about their

first date pub's smooch

and cuddle moods of inchoate romance,

must be musing over their hookah bar times

of lolling lounge and laughter,

fellas bullying and bragging,

feeling the scenario's hazy fizz,

while the undulating concentric

coned smoke circles

tells us the party wayward photo frame's

affable capture of mirth and gay,

just like this picture's ray kissed hairs

of lovely tango curls,

groovy waves and love jazz,

just as this gloomy dusk and the cafe brew

revels her insides with brimming feels

of passion & life,

kissing her chill evening moments with

slice of joy and cup of love!

10
salsa, jazz and the fiesta of love ..

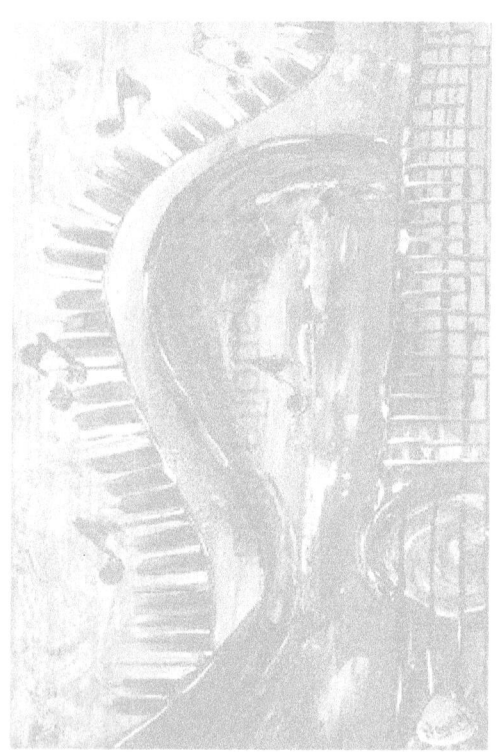

Salsa, jazz and the fiesta ..

Guess the poster is trying to capture

the delirious and jazzy mind

of a lover lad's merry over his dance

with his love on their prom perhaps,

with the vibrant and grooving strings of bass

equally falling ecstatically on the swifty play of pianist,

to the rapid salsa of the sensuous romance

taking its stance at its deep from their lovely little hearts,

for the moves of smile picking up over the dance of lasting tango,

toeing for the beats and the rhythm of passion

inlaid in exhilarating fiesta of lovers delight,

the screech, and the scratch, of red guitars' brush overs

might go in a wave with the dance of salsa

on the tunes of loud and high jazzy scores

embossing its beats and rhythm

and the elegant curves just as portrayed

by the guitar edge yodeling for the scene's gloss,

the raying out strokes of the black and white cords

should probably try to depict their colourful moves

of freestyle with kisses and rushes

over each other's body for the spark

of techno electric beats

to their augmenting high pitch woofing out feel of elation,

and yellow shades of plaster in the backdrop

tries to outlay a fire may be

just as the dreams of love that has got engraved between them,

just as the passionate burning dance floor

over where they are grooving

on to the flying brews of high flowing jazz,

to the passionate beats of love and

the striking flawless rhythm of glowing wonder,

for their flaming fiesta of exuberant vibes

on the floor of romantic ecstacy,

pushing and pulling and hoping over

kissing smooching and smashing on

for a party of blast,

on their never ending tango of sexy salsa...

melancholy of a mystique medley dream .. & other selected poetry

11
a red silhouetted
romance ..

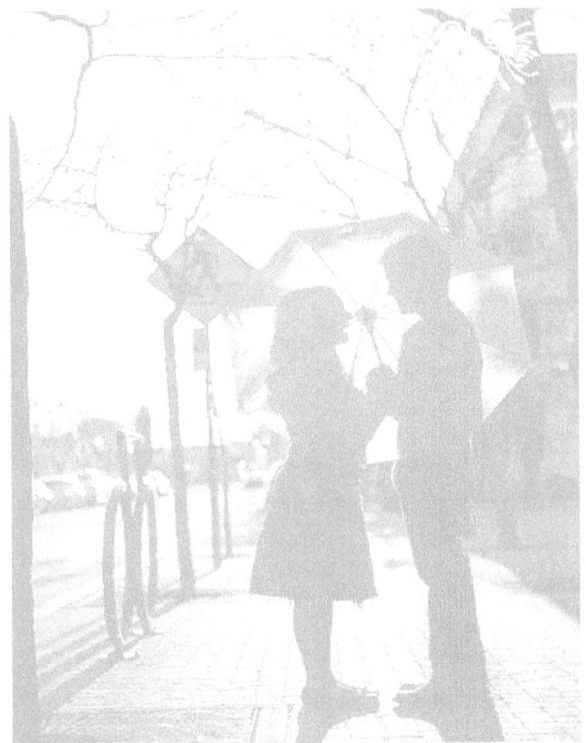

a red silhouetted romance ..

Perhaps a sunday's lovely summer morning,

with kissing smooth rays from the sun,

and almost deserted streets

and a closed up place more or less,

a seemingly late-night like morning surrounding,

choco look lover boy running high,

moving quickly to catch over his girl

with that excitement and

a oozing out, delicately choco coated,

a vanilla sauced cakie chill delight,

the cheer and glow of the young heart's love afresh

and his scintillating feel of embossed teenage rhythm

bassing all through,

just like when the paris seem when it sizzles

while the lovers seek their blissful merry kissing

dancing and singing in the rain of love,

like the sound of cello stringing over the mind

so passionately grooving for the time to be relished with his girl, *the long chatty and slow walk,*

with hand in hand that clasps tightly at times

and a slow losing hold some times with a slight waver

inside the lightly scared teen heart over the ideas of love and future,

and that snailing little fear

of getting caught by some neighbor's eye,

talking about the day that went by

with the titanic romance of jack and rose on hbo,

while he pulls her back from the stern,

while they muse about the art,

while they intimately move over each other

as the lovers looking into their twinkling eyes

with that tiny little feel of the unsaid inching inside,

and almost the rest of plot to follow,

for the time of laughter kicking up

and the mildly blending in intimate desires,

they continue chatting,

about the unfinished chemistry assignment

thats gonna screw em up the following day,

about the cute little eyes of the puppy

his uncle gifted him recently,

about her newly shopped shiny high heels,

over their love, their days ahead and blah blah blah

just to groove in with the time syncing into the moment

to make their secret weekend tryst of elating exuberance

and the exquisitely painted feel of the first love,

the first experience of high spirited teen romance,

a ever stretched and a never ending adorable time

of choco love delicacy pictured behind the kissy-red love veil

over the everlasting sweetened drama

on the shot of the red silhouetted romance!

12

a surreal night's sextain ..

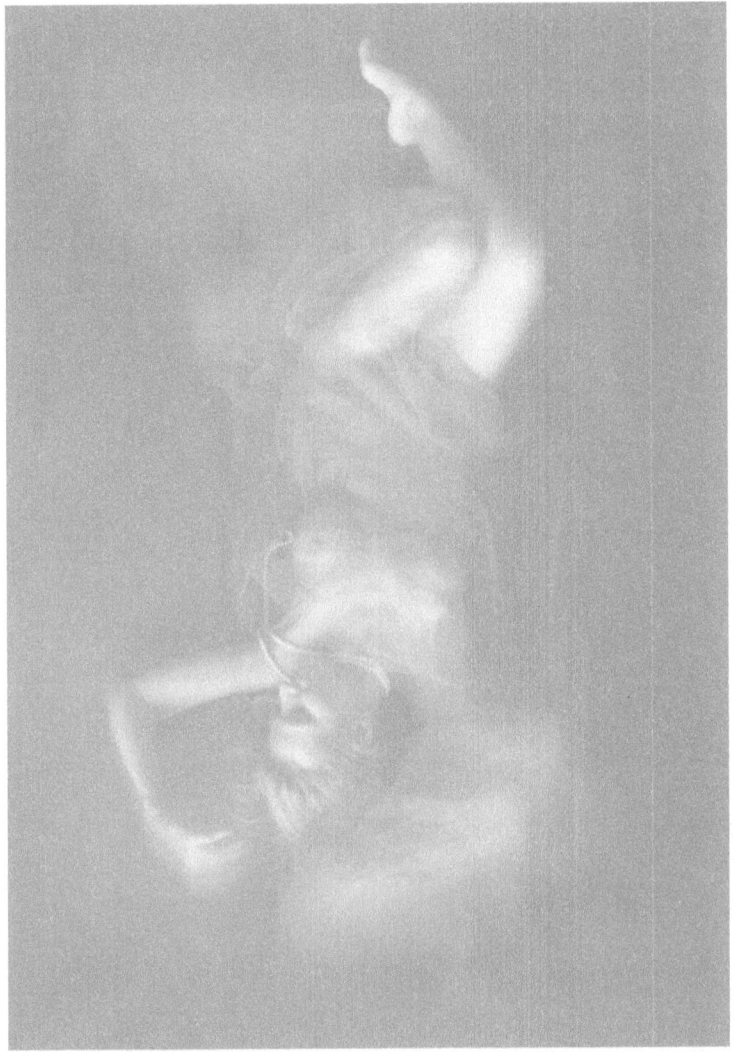

a surreal night's sextain ..

such a flawless skin so fair and white,

her long dishevelled hair undulating

in the zephyr around,

raising the mood and the desires

of the loner moon's midnight,

such beautiful curves of the femme fatale

call's aphrodite arousing,

while you kiss and caress

those lovely breasts that oozes out the milk

of the feminine floral springs

seducing you to the sensual

embrace of soothing warmth,

the feminine sensual intimacy

behind the erotica angels' coalesced ritual

amongst those seducing incandescent magnolia,

the sacrament's glowing fervour inducing the amour,

alongside those iridescent flora

that would perhaps even arouse folks

to gleaming blithe of the lewdland's forgotten erotica,

the wee hours' sensual apparition is so queer

glooming the space around like that murky haze

of the morning fog immersing the loner moon

in a marvellous rivulet,

converging the lucency of love

that is glazing in her moonlight serenade,

unravelling the song of seduction

with interludes of deeply intimate aria,

the lyric of lust, the sextain and the mood behind

the lambent moonlight dip,

hovering around in her intimacy's lustre,

the slit of his blade as the dipping blood

kissing the moon satiating her darker secrets beneath,

the slithering red lanes of splatter

sliding down her maroon orgy,

underneath the blood kissed moon so white,

so wild is her surreal night's crimson fulgere

soaked in his blade's lucency,

as the spirit of casanova glades by the loner moon's aria.

13
everything that ain't no dark

everything that ain't no dark ..

The lovely gleams of heavenly light are in a shimmering glaze,

that seems to dwelve inside this space

like the golden glades of the rapenzel's fortress window.

Through the gap between the thin drapes

of seducing patina they sneak in,

so prevailing and so brimming,

they gleam the place with

plethora of love behind its effulgence.

Like a celestial rivulet they shimmer inside,

blending in with the relishing streams

of unlikely irradiance that accumulates the surrounding

with everything that ain't no dark.

The scintillating streams of the celestial rivulet

paints the colors of glades and love

so vivid and so prolonging.

The light is love and love is light

says everything that ain't no dark.

The celestial rivulet seems to paradigm a love stream,

the path of impeccable streams

of passion tracing its art of dwelling

in ardent fervor and innate lustre

that bounds its refulgent crux

and the subtle nuances behind.

The streaming rays that seems to

restoreth the continuum's aural debliss,

plunging inside with blooms,

brightness and everything that ain't no dark.

Its ambient songs of arduous fervor

bringsforth the sensual effervescence

amidst the stream's daze of tiny photons

and starry specks of love and lustre

that seems to river its glades

of such unlikely fulgere

holding onto its niche of sheen,

alongside its streams of myriad

miniature crescents that seems

to radiate the light of love

so unparalleled and so true.

The space possesses such strange

tenacity within that could unknot, lift

and resuscitate the beholder no matter

the darkness or its intensity,

though it seems quite obscure

to the beholder while tracing back

to its initial source or its origin.

The light is love and love is light

says everything that ain't no dark.

14
art unconventional

art conventional ..

modern day art works often queer and vague,

makes people keep guessing on its strange ideas

and obscure content, sometimes plain and simple,

sometimes harsh and loud

and at other times even bizzare and boring.

Be it a graphite on paper or a subtle monochrome

or oil on canvas and other art forms

Be it a clay sculpt or a gadget illustration

abstract and vague the content goes

modern and liberal the substance goes.

Bright colors used inside a painting

tend to attract a person's eye pulling him

inside its pigment's spread

and alluring him into its varying colors over the canvas

more predominantly than the dull shades.

the loud animations behind these artistic rendering

It's simple outline sometimes of a minimalist

It's adept craft behind a cubist

Or a eerie allegory of a dali's

in the postmodern arena

tries to capture the artist's mind behind the idea

in a subtle sense converging its attributed nuances

over the thought or the idea's expressions,

In eloquent style and metaphorical connotations,

That you hardly grasp in naked eye.

Expressionism portrays the logic in abstract ideas

in vivid content substantially

while trying to gather

the artist's mind behind his work

through bright shades of symbolism

and possibly even beyond its contour

of conveying the theme that lies underneath.

Whatever the theme an artist might decide to deliver

he expresses it in a style rather

that lies beneath obscurity

and conveying the notion inside in vague strokes of arcs or curves,

brushing it out in loud pigments

creating a banner that shouts out

the message he wants to deliver

the theme he wants to convey,

more often in colors that are not dim

in high tone while outlining the theme

that are more often again going to lie

beyond a layman's reach.

Post modern artistry makes an artist feel free,

makes an artist feel he is aboard

the liberal bounds of his own courtyard

to convey his artform to the outside world,

it shouts out loud,

it cries out the pain,

it voices the world

and provides a subtle platform to express

his views and theme,

wherein the creator is left free

in depicting his notions,

be it in a minimalistic sense

or say a surreal portraiture of an artform

and so on.

Unconventional art and Postmodern era have liberalized folks

and their work in a seamless approach

of delivering an artform

and the way we have evolved

in the modern era entails

these platforms as the art medium

for connecting with the world

needs the progressive sync with the people's mind

and perceptions and the way he conceives an idea

and the people's attitude these days,

in a augmented sense in its growth.

And more on freeing the artist too

without any constraints in his expressions and ideas,

while trying to convey his elements

behind a logic in a contemporary note and style.

15
kiss of the war ..

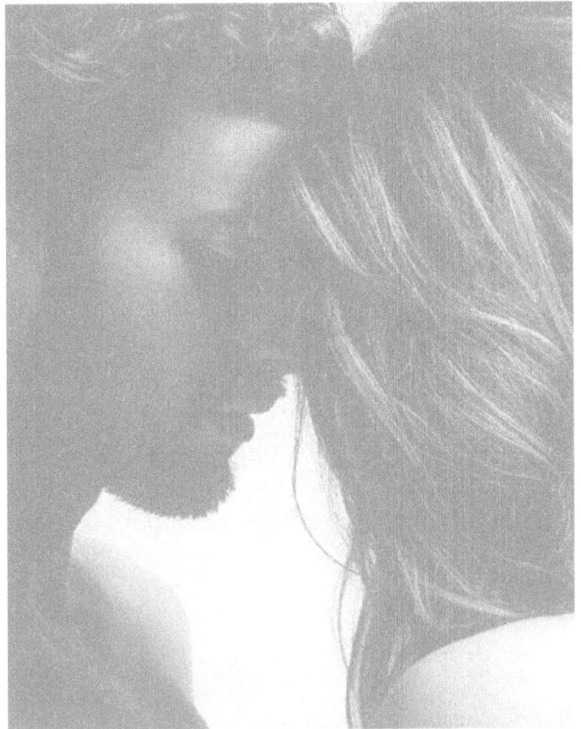

kiss of the war ..

A beautiful capture, shot may be after a final love making,

the next day which the war hero is gonna get back

to his base after his break,

his sadly gloomed dull face leaned over his lady's face

with lovingly flaming hairs,

tells the story behind,

the fading out zeal owing to separation

may be could have taken its toll

coupled with the thought over his loneliness

for months together into the days of wretched war

out there in the forsaken wilderness missing his beloved,

losing out her love,

but with the pride inside his heart

over him being the part

of carrying his nation's safeguard and honour,

still the almost closed eyes thinking about his waring ways perhaps,

those days in the woods and

feeling the deeply roughened earth inside

fighting out the enemies with blasts and shots and fire all around,

running over the ground dodging hits

and experiencing deafening ammos

throwing you away hitting hard breaking bones,

with gore bloodshed all over and

unlookably pierced flesh bodily insides

wounded & dead soldiers' corpses lying around,

even might take on a bullet on the arm one bad day

with a pain so very aching over the body

while a heart of passion and valour

and the sheer dogged spirit

on the mission with the grittily loaded mighty strength

of a thousand tuskers put together,

taking the man through his objective ways

hitting over the mission-run's triumph

thats been waiting not so far away,

and all the more getting back to his nest

over a victory to taste his scotchy romance,

to feel that eternal kiss of his love...

16
melancholy of a mystique medley war ..

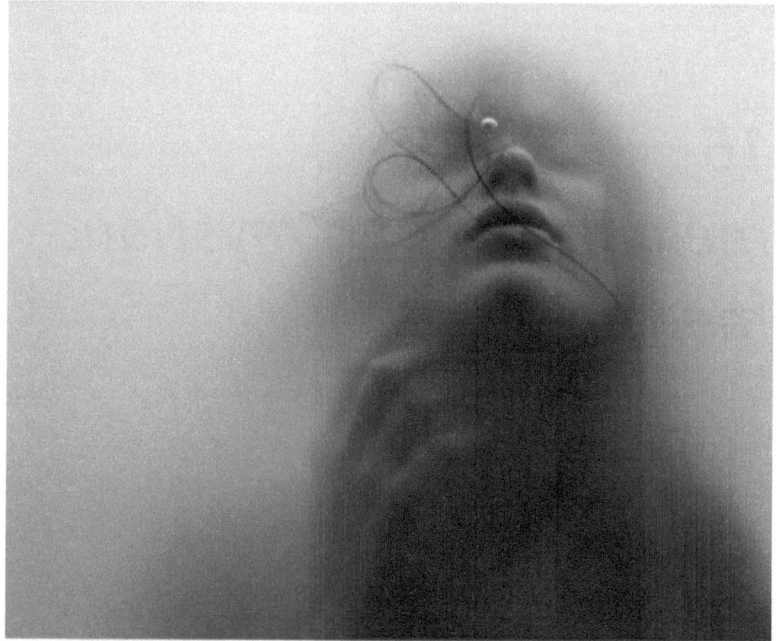

melancholy of a mystique medley dream ..

Its while in the early dawn amidst the dense fog

in the coldest of the mystical circumstantial continuum,

where in you feel no inertia around,

when you feel yourself just like another strand,

as in midst of other myriad similar undulating fibres

of beautiful feminine floweral springs,

to tune the melancholy of the medley dream

that takes its stance inside your dramatically zephyred

inner darker shades of oozing drizzles,

that might have taken its inspirational origin

out of the imaginative fictitious fibral fragmentation

inside the mind's discreet veiled vision

of high passion and kissing, over with a sense of tranquil mysticism

immersed inside the delusional ides of the translucent

perceptive focus right into the solo eternal entity

of the myriad feminine strand field,

of that absolutely cold and fluidly smoked up

gravity defying space of the deeper sight's intuitive musing.

The feminine strand field's swaying and swinging reclusive dreamers,

who miss their love continuum when demigrating

out of their mystical land in the existential realism,

which the mystique lords of the femina strand field's inebriative exalting,

view just as a mere space that lacks the source of the firing eternal love

and a meaning less continuum for these reclusive stranders

inside in here of their alternative contemplative delusional mystique land

and just that the primal originative space of realism for these men

exists just due to lack of their higher elevating secretions

and escalating substabces of inebriative shades.

The Mystique Lords of the femina strand fields induce

the strands to kiss their dreams,

brewing it right inside their mind's existential spots,

who feel that these highly floated fibril fragments

of their internally originating elements of brew cloud clogging

into their strand space's surrounding foggie fluids of solacing accumulations.

Filling up of these solace accumulative space

rather the volume of reclusive strand's dream fill brews,

entails the Mystique Lords' touch on a individualistic look over, by their mind fibril

elements compositive aspects

of emotional slots that makes them to perceive

the strand femme fatale's inner consisting fibres,

through which the Lords fill up the solace space's foggie fluid

to make the strands float inside the consoling heart's liquid,

to feel the eternally existing Love,

for lifting up the strand in their low insides

to contemplate them with the exalted serenic atmosphere

of mysticism and to thoroughly immerse them

into ever flowing instantaneously fountained heart liquid's

intimacy, love, passion and to kiss up their yearn

with the mystique land's spell to excite

and tranquil their minds to the immortal contemplation

of their soul's unaching phenomena ..

melancholy of a mystique medley dream .. & other selected poetry

17
walking endless ..

walking endless ..

Seems a lady lost in love,

amidst her sad floating thoughts

on love and longing, with aching feelings

from the insides of her heart,

looking for the way that seems so unclear

with the road that she has to travel

on lying in a pretty much out of bounds vicinity, walking over a

clueless track,

a aimless wander into the vast desert

of forsaken love with no spot of tenderness,

with a sad and dull mind and loads of pain

burdened over a broken heart thats been trying

to hold over her beautifully framed up blissful love engraved

from her times

while she had been framing up her fairy tale romance, dreaming

about her merry love

for the eternal ever after,

seems all those dreams of ardent passion

and beautiful days of love

woven from the inner core of her heart

have been shattered even before

she tried to convey her love,

perhaps the stint here could be

she would'nt have been in a slightest of an idea
about her lover's girlfriend, until a while ago.

Fate some times plays a cruel game
of unangelic tricks trying to collapse the plot
and shattering the dreams of a person
totally to a solo aimless wander
of woeing pathos getting its tune
from the mind's distinct little space
oozing out from a pretty lower voice of aches
and its deeply sad lyrics
of a ode over a love
over a heartfelt longing
over a dreams of years,
trying to reminisce the frames of the times,
when she was actually painting all those dreams inside her head
with flying colors,
while she had been building over her fortress of love and joy on
the man of her dreams,
and while she'd been sculpting her days of future
with her man's embrace from the clay of her heart.

Seems the wrecked-she is in search
of a solace least to a little bit,
in that vast wilderness of desert so void and dark,

so hot and burning,

just like the brutal fate that stashed away

all her dreams passion and love,

playing the evil hand anti-scripting her fairytale

to a endless story,

stealing away her man,

destructing her beautifully dreamed up fortress

of heaven, and stashing out her destiny itself. Perhaps, the lady

in red,

walking over the waves of heat with stolid face

and devastated head,

and over her inside emptiness

of desert sand's burns,

sadly seems to be living soulless ... seems to be breathing lifeless

... seems to be walking endless ...

18
half a soul's labyrinth ..

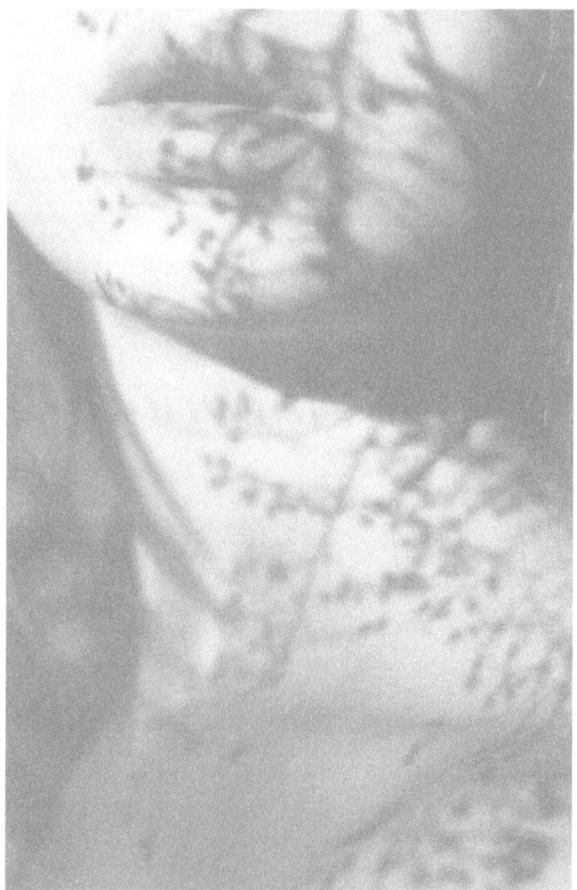

half a soul's labyrinth ..

while looking to manoeuvre inside those days

of wretched inner tiredness lacking the substantial elements

of cardinal signing in the soul's half,

over its lack of the tool for the signing groove

or even at times its gonna place inside a dry and dull shell

of void where you even gonna lack the ink.

The diva of charisma here seems on the look out for a deviation

from her slow manoeuvre ways that has crept

into her lonely darker pages thats been found blank,

rather the pages seem broody and bugged up

in a milder tones of sepia.

Those beautiful mild pink lips of the erotic charm's impeccable portrayal

and the forms of the flawless finesse skin

below her lovely lower face of the cupid angels' queen,

tries to convey her yearn over her enigmatic times

of a flowerless garden, a colorless flower,

a pigmentless color, her half soul's stature

of desiccated rusts over her dubious and devious ways

of solo aches like a music without sound,

while its vibes innately lagging over its media

for its path of traverse to surround the continuum

on a holistic spread which could only perhaps drive its purpose

to its destined reach of making the feel inside the heart's sensing heeds.

Her sepiatic tones of pages are dark and brown

dipped inside the dry and dirt loveless preparing potion from the pulps,

as the tiny reflective dry stems of sticks

devoid of its fullest tenderness trying to evade her

from her light's discreet inner glitter

by the instantaneously reverting back breeze's slender kiss,

leaving her off clueless in the wilderness.

yet if she could intercept herself with her line's destined run

without the evil manoeuvring times of falsifying turns

just like the one she's into,

in the riddlingly unfortunate present of labyrinth

and if she could really paint herself with the flowers

of the garden of love eden's enchanting paradise,

and if only the diva could muse out of her slow twisting manoeuvres

to the eternal charm of her half soul's scripture

right from the ink of their hearts,

the innate bliss of her life's garden

would never lack its charming blooms...

19
scent of the scripting papyrus ..

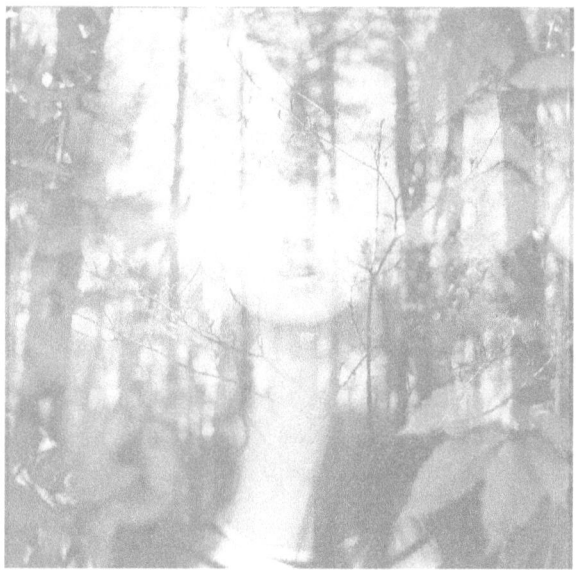

scent of the scripting papyrus ..

eside the burnt ashes of the night's camp fire,

while swaying inside the intoxicated grey mind's delusional insights,

into the deep and dark woods, waving around alone

to capture the outer world's light inside,

to feel the beautiful scenic nature's expansive embrace

right through the earth's firming touch

and its relishing love of multitude higher greens' tender grace,

you tend to lose yourself deep into your heart's diluting contemplations,

with the insides wheeling its mind's emotional attributes,

while you read over those aging parchments of inconsolable ache

engraved from the lost love of the eluding phases,

inking its soul's lamentations.

The Scripture read might pull you down on a mourning low,

even to the nadir of the sad feel's crying ride on a onus rhyme

tuning out its impactual melodrama

to the higher enacting substance of a classic's attire,

where in the sinking blues floating over your life's sensual posters, *hovers you around through the nostalgic unerasable frames*

of de angelic woods' love lady,

to delude around the vast open's panoramic hallucinations

augmenting the paranormal sensations of inebriative dizzying reactions

in the inner core space of emotional juncture

which might disturb its flattened sync on a distorting mild tremors.

Like the cold wind's intuitive seductions,

from the wild woods' picture of affectionate embrace

trying to shade you around over your painful gruel,

to console the blackened heart's grieving sorrow,

the lady gets you down to exfoliate you

with the kiss of woods' higher greens,

when you quench in your arid venom aches

wiping the angelic lady woods' tear roll down.

Witnessing a slowly manoeuvring array

of flying translucent images from the engraved paintings

of the holy ghost lady woods' delusional ride back,

mired right on the inner minds

to lift out of the existential illusory plight

of unforgettable pain and blank hues

of a aching love's musive walk through the woods

of darker black inking,

times could take the loner lad's senses to the abyss of sadness,

with a stoned souring throat and bitter raw spirit,

the extremely broken you might experience

the unusual second presence of a holy cloud's mystique being,

breezing toward you its hallucinative soothing voices

in the deserted scene around to enclave you

onto its space of floatingly reviving brighter flow

to the vitalising paints of exhilarating chords,

for the dozingly wretched you to flight out

of the black and browned ground

of the parchment odes' romantic woes and to confront

you on with a sensual convergence

over the drenching will of the divine intervention,

immersing you on to the deblackening pond of the holy roots,

shielding on with the woods'

delusionally hovering love of mystical touch,

whirling on the lad with the smell

of the new dawn's scripting papyrus...

20
de wandering soul ..

.

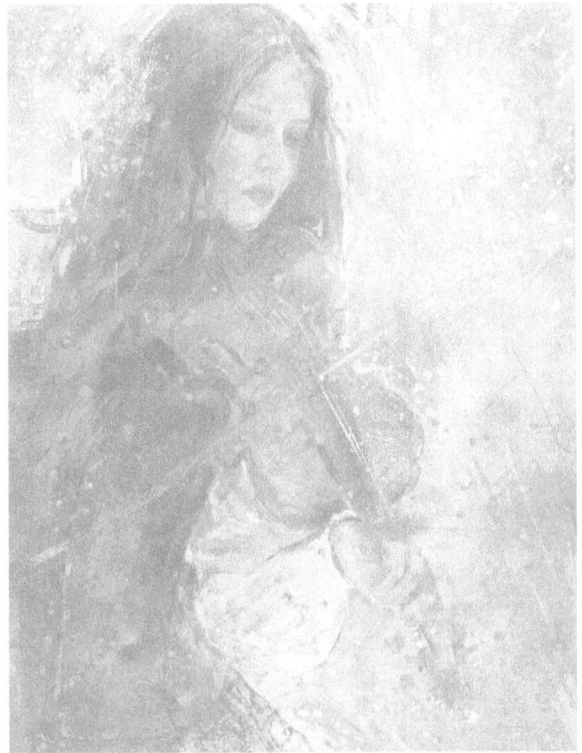

de wandering soul ..

its the stringing girl,

seemingly away from her love,

looking for the tunes to play her

sadly gloomed circumstantial mind evading time

in the absence of her man who has been far off,

framed out there in the cold breezy night

of isolation's dullness in the backdrop

with white spatters of snow

and dip brush slight swings

of wandering soul in the night,

aching love at the dark,

pains of voidness all over,

with chillness of the snow kissing her face

and the cold blowing wind embracing her tight

that has got its trajectory apparently from her tale's hero,

the eyes that look low on to the strings

she is grooving into,

for the sad tunes she is scripting on,

that lovely red lips starting to turn a bit dry

with that lack of the so yearned moisture may be,

and the highlighted blue-greened violin

trying to portray musically

the bass-sour stringed plot of her

mildly insomniac wander

with that sad emptiness lacking her spirit

unlike her times of love aria

and perhaps its picturing to play on

the lack of deeply yearned dreams

that she'd cry for right now,

which could only save her heart breezing

her over to her man,

waning her off the blue woes...

21
stoned times of lone fallacy ..

stoned times of lone fallacy ..

*The roads are calm and quite desolated with almost none
around in the surrounding. its a rainy night though not much of
a pour, seemingly after the showers have subsided, with none
other than this lonely girl walking all alone in the wee hours of
the night. Seems like she is tired and feeble out of the recent
breakup perhaps, making her feel low and dull taking in the
scene's pathos behind, the sorta heavy road she is moving about
in blues. Its the kind of a night that you are feeling all messy in
pain and pangs of love, that you would actually relate to the
sort of avril lavign crooning yeehs and yaahs in the sense of
missing that someone, in the insecure feels of losing him and the
circumstance that is so mean leading her to a road of bizarre
with all the vague questions in their relationship's current
stature.*

*Her sober head and
the slumber mood
in some aching
dilemma makes her
feel all dizzy,*

*as if its spinning
and spinning,*

round and round,

in slow sluggish

whirls of void,

spinning around again

sulking inside in

some stoned times

of lone fallacy,

as if the lyric is

lacking its music,

an opera sans its

libretto,

and an orchestra

sans its strings,

trying to stumble

her in a bizarre

road of

aimless wander,

in a byzantine

route of

vague hassles,

in a vertigo of

loveless labyrinth ..

22
aching love of a romantic ..

aching love of a romantic ..

a heart broken lover lad's poetical capture

of his mind frame perhaps,

his blur vision of

abstrusive path that lay ahead of him,

after that long wretched and

weary ride on his horse down

the tracks of his flashing past over

his lady's first sight as he

steered beside those majestic mountains

of the love gods,

his unerasable moments of

ardent amour and fervent ardour

shared with her,

that first lock over lips

as he veered on dark green woods

of hidden yearnings looking

for the fountain of youth's intimacy,

that burning warmth of scintillating

passion's first spread

they dwelved into on that

late wee hours of the

night before sunrise,

as he cruised over the bridge

right on that elegant waters

of clear cupid streams,

the indelible letters of love

they shared on their ravens

that pictured their pain

poetically inking up their

minds of glooming sadness

on the days of isolation,

while he had been moving along

the exquisite flowers greens and

colours of their woven dreams

over their fabric of youth's lustre,

and riding on into the deep woods

over the gruelling routes of sands

stones and thorns tearing the winds

chasing the storms

embracing the sanddust

with his beard face and

a wartime evening attire

with a bearing mind of his

lady's refutative disappearance,

turning down enervated,

looking out for the eluding mirage

thats evidently deceptive

eluding his eyes all the while

and searching over his ecstatic rainbow

that debloomed out of her woman

suddenly in the present midway of his plot

trying to deceive his senses,

with that present emptiness' raw feel

of sour inching up his throat's

acid slit ache rooted directly from

his lady's ameobatic turn

she slipped over him

forgetting the days of their

ever relishable romance,

the words of promise and depth lettered through,

and the lasting holy love they shared for.

with that prevailing voidic

inside's lack of heart

he kneels down on the riverside,

after his soul tiring cruise of

days together with engraved sadness inside,

drenched down in deep aches

of his lady's inconsolable refutation and denial

and craving in vain for that

last bit of a quantum solace to the least,

cant standing the persent stature of time...

23

pangs, pathos and vodka shots ..

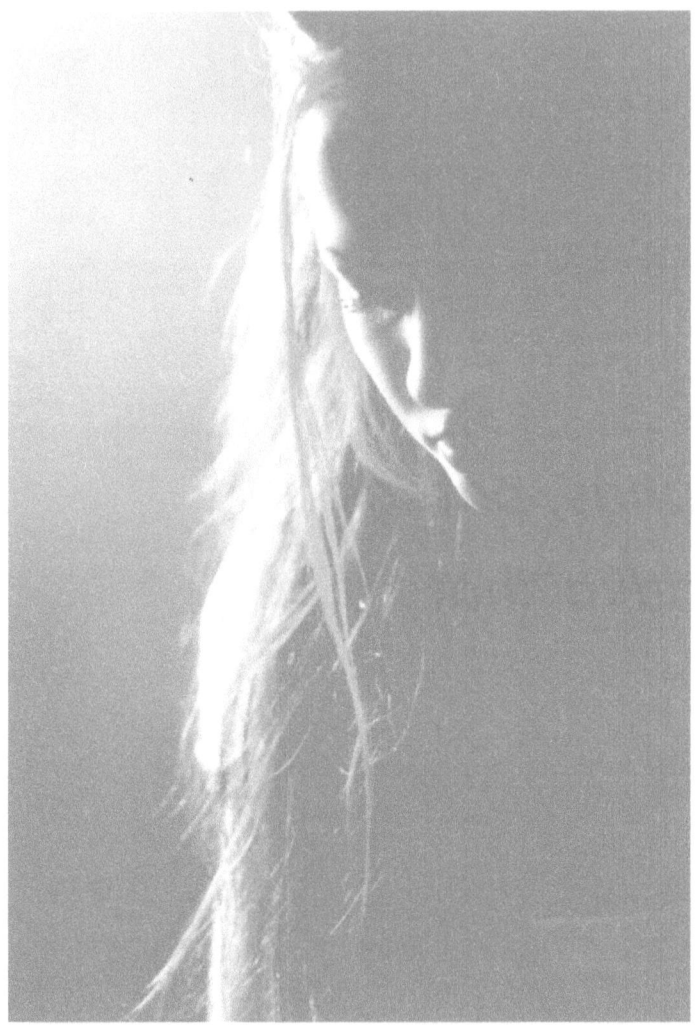

pangs, pathos and vodka shots ..

its a dull and gloomy friday evening,

the sky is grey above and the clouds are brewing along,

with winds blowing slightly harder.

With lovely undulating pony tailed brown hairs, fair face,

dressed in a tight tee and jacket ,

she is quickly getting down the stairs with a tired head.

Seems like she is slightly out of sorts, her dull face

Suggests her inner tiredness, perhaps the recent lack of her beau's

connection could be the reason indeed, not a single call

in a fortnight's time, no messages nor pokes or chats.

She is moving swiftly by the trees

unusually noticing its close line up

and the dark black barks so hard, so ridged,

standing tall alongside in this hazy dusk,

in her way to parking lot to catch up another mate,

and get a drive back home or might even think about a pub
around.

Stuck in the midway by something, startled a bit

and taking a couple of quicker strides,

she looks harder at that black car

to get a clearer sight and ends up slowing down

getting hold of a tree's bark.

trapped by the mood's pathos may be,

as she sees her beau pulling in another girl

kissing by the window, she gets down slowly

by the tree and sits there leaning on the bark

preoccupied with all tangled thoughts inside.

She is muddled inside with a unclear mind

and mildly creeping in pangs of void,

that seems to hauntingly slither her insides

slow and quiet.

it dwelves in her insides like the thin crawling

worms of voidic black that might

seem to subtly seize her whole,

as the claws of octopus which could

swiftly strech it arm to clench and grasp,

clasping it in no time all of a sudden,

spreading its worms of void all around

creeping and crawling.

She is equally taken in by the mood's pathos,

swinging in mildly, pulling her low and dull,

while trying to reflect her birdie blues.

Its is dark all around and the place is

almost deserted with only her

musing by the tree and sulking under it,

and none else to be seen in the sight around.

a muse of a lone lady, sad and dull,

as she tries to gather herself

out of her mood's blue hues.

Being haunted by the pathos and pangs,

she is almost hovering around in the rain literally,

lost in her blues, mired by her thoughts

and creeping in fear,

along with the mundane's weariness.

She reaches her apartment late and feels like

her drive back home has taken thrice its usual time

while dragging her ride so slow in lapse,

over and over in the whirls of turns around the blocks,

spinning and spinning in whirls and turns of daze,

stretching her ride in her mind's maze,

inside her intoxicated sulking mind

inside her spinning head,

post their stop by in a local pub and

owing to the vodka shots' aftermath.

She stands in front of her room's mirror

Keeping herself apathetic to her pathos,

under the flickering light that is yet to be replaced,

its light its dark in a flash, its light its dark,

its light, its dark it flickers sporadically,

she observes herself so indifferently.

She tries to pour another shot of vodka

from the bottle of absolut in her table,

but ends up breaking the glass dropping it down.

She takes a shot directly from the bottle.

on a spinning high she is,

stoned and apathetic.

reluctantly she moves to the balcony

to get some different air,

to get some other feeling,

to get some different light,

to get some other noise or blare to the least.

Standing in the balcony,

She gets that different feeling

Of the open outside.

Sees all the lights from the

road's cabs and vehicles,

the beam and the glare.

Slowly closing her eyes

hears its sound, its noise

and the blare.

She feels the outside air.

She feels the outside.

Its wee hours of the midnight,

Thirty passed two.

She is still awake lying in the floor,

hazy and high,

as another shot of vodka gets in.

her mobile plays charlie's,

we don't talk anymore.

intoxication is helping her in keeping herself off

from the present pangs and pathos.

the stoned she feels the silence of the night

standing in the terrace floor,

while her inside space's light

still goes on and off flickering,

light and dark, flashing on and off.

24

on a lonely winter's night ..

on a lonely winter's night ..

Everything is so dark in front of me

in this lonely winter night,

and its utterly desserted in this darker side of wee hours

with none you could find amidst

this cold lonely winter night.

I am lying beneath these kissing waters,

musing in the midnight,

stoned and intoxicated feeling the gag inside,

the stolid me trying to embark

on a queer muse over the darkness

in front of me and the tiny scattered dots

of white sheen inside this vast spread

of dark on a lonely winter night.

Am i seeing a hunter, is it,

is that the hunter's grouping,

as they call them in the mythology of greek.

He is holding his weapon raised right above his head,

and like a demon he stands,

so fierce and wild could you capture his eyes,

so obdurate and staunch could you perceive his stature,

the triplet in the middle of his body,

the three dots spaced between equal distance,

the sign should say of this enigmatic creature's identity,

the hunter's triplet as they call it

in the myth in this northern sky.

Lying in the gentle waves

I am musing in the midnight

upon this vast sea of darkness

holding its dots of white sheen so queer and so lull,

alongside this chill breeze of obscure urges

wherein you could nt figure the dark or its dots,

the way you would have wanted to,

could neither figure the enigma inside

nor its nonchalant random interpretations

or perhaps its illusory ideas behind,

in a inebriated mind's swing by on a lonely winter's night.

25

on est dessus garde .. part i

on est dessus garde .. part i

the crux behind the core is seriously unknown.

None knows about its legend and its sacred peak, no not anyone.

The obscurity on its composition is quite apparent

owing to its archaic secrecy and age long legacy,

and they are alongside this arena for ages,

holding intact its primordial hidden myth

and standing as true keepers of its flame.

They are up behind in guarding it from the apparition, evil and the bad,

that are crudely diverging the arena from its angelic coalescence,

its ethereal goodness.

Thousands of angels, myriad guards are there around

the core's enormity holding along its irradiance,

burning along in its glow,

dancing through its denser rays and shimmering glades.

They stay around

they stay around all through,

shielding the arena with such indomitable spirit

and unconquerable might, such valor and the vigor

holding along with their inner light,

so fierce and so destined they are,

so mighty and so ardent they seem.

None have seen them sleep no not one,

none have seen them eat no not anyone,

none have seen them cease their guard not anyone,

no not even for seconds,

ceaselessly they guard around

they guard around all through,

untiring spirits and unconquerable might

maketh their fortress,

such warriors of fearless eyes and obdurate stance

maketh their battalion.

You could see mammoth lions that are so ferocious,

you could see tuskers with such rigor,

two headed hounds of such big grey eyes,

you could see white horses of incredible strength

that you might not have seen elsewhere so unique of the battalion.

Their elegant armors are up in their arms shielding them from enemy aim,

their firing blades are waiting to behead the enemy at front,

'kill, kill.. kill em all' is the slogan, 'for any evil at sight.. '.

'We the warriors of the core, standing here to protect

and safegaurd the arena, with all thy might

and all thy power, we stay around

we stay around days and nights,

we stay around all through ceaselessly.

Let our armours shield us from our enemies,

we re not gona allow anyone to cross your shield, no not one,

let our swords behead our enemies at sight,

we re not gona let any evil to evade our blades, no not one.

Lets slaughter every last one of them.

we the keepers of the flame are standing here to protect

and safegaurd the arena with all thy might and all thy power,

we stay around we stay around days and nights,

we stay around all through, ceaselessly,

we the parade of thousand angels and myriad gaurds,

we the loyal gaurdians of the core,

we the core battalion.

on est dessus garde,

on est dessus garde.'

26
on est dessus garde
part ii

on est dessus garde .. part ii

The keepers of the flame or the gaurdians of the mighty battalion,

have never eaten anything they say,

nor those mysterious guards have closed their eyes to sleep

the myth holds, oh believe me they say it in the myth.

They dwell as half human and half angel,

the angels of the arch who are so destructive and determined,

all eyes on their guard, so watchful

and so dreadful they are,

with a holy mystique demi god's might and such strange fierce power,

so unique of this arch guard battalion,

they guard on, they guard on.

Weapons of blades and swords they cut their enemies with,

the spears and the arrows they peirce their evil with,

oh, blink of an eye thats all it takes,

he gets in tearing the wind, he slays,

oh, blink of an eye thats all it takes,

he vanishes leaving the foe in gore.

Oh thee, none can save you,

at his sight if you re his foe.

Oh thee, dont turn to his side,

for nothing can save you from his fury

and wrath if you re evil.

The secret of the crux is unknown,

none knows about its mystery,

for thousands guard its hidden secrets and seal their holy intricacies,

for ten thousands protect and safeguard its arena

and the most profound core, and its underlying myth, the immortal saga.

For centuries they are in guard the thousand holy angels

and myriad warriors, protecting and bounding their core in shield,

oh beware thou enemies,

for sans breathe the guard could live,

oh beware thou enemies,

you ll never know when or how the guard will take you on,

a blink thats all it takes,

a fraction's blink,

for sans even a form the guard dwells and exists,

through the wind's black hallows they fly and hide.

with untiring keeness and unpenetrable armour they guard on,

immersed in the black aura of the angelic pond's dip

they guard on amidst those gleams and glades of the enigmatic core,

they guard on, guard on.

'We fight for the core, we protect and safeguard it... ', shouts the leader,

' we the parade of thousand angels andd myriad guards,

we the loyal guardians,

we the core battalion,

on est dessus garde.

on est dessus garde.'

27
the falcon traverse

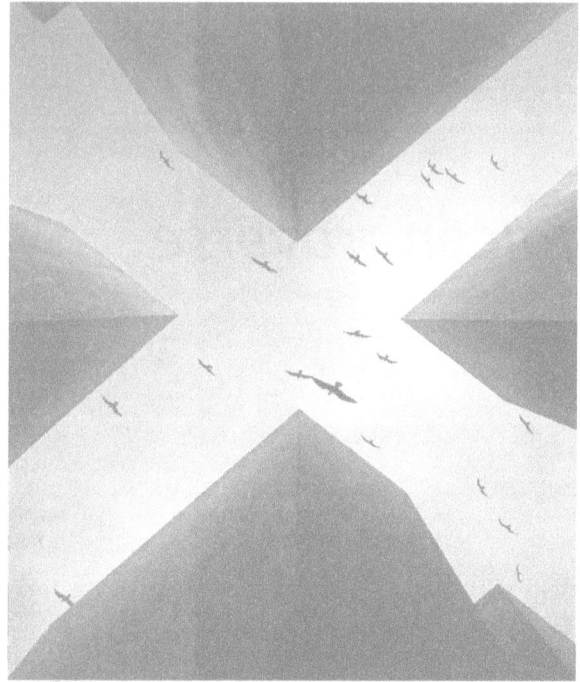

the falcon traverse ..

Viewing things on a scale which you wouldn't rather usually see,

takes that augmented stride inside your mind

on a elevated level in a larger zone of macro aligning.

The eye of a falcon has got that critical

and great potential of a ariel view on its escalated top's hawk eye

from the skies to hit in track with the prerequisite

for fronts framing aspect either on the larger scale

in the timeline flow or the certain limit on the period lane

with a focus over a specific concerned theme of scope.

The primal elements in the delicate framing

of the look ahead structure in any concern

have to be in this preliminary view look over,

further to which the placing of blocks in the macro aligning mat

could take its stance wherein the side-line substance

of framing structure like time line push-ons

on the block mat and track laying essentials

between the blocks of the macro aligning,

and augmented with the other matters

of fore manipulative contour outlining,

could be assigned to hawk over

the fascinating mat framing arena

over the lateral falcon eye's

exhilarating perspective stream way

for the holistic boundary approach

to the destined aim rather goals

in the taken matter of generic outlook

along with its innate structural inherent blocks

of the concerned avenue area.

A smooth urban ride of the fog less clear road's knack,

and with the tactics of a dark falcon higher light's,

traited up as in a watchful protector,

a silent falcon guardian,

and filmed on with a framing embodiment

of a mighty orientation,

could logically enhance the roads attached

to the perfect driving way

of framing up the macro aligning mat

for a splendid cruise on a beautiful picturesque traverse.

.

28
the sacred luminance

the sacred luminance ..

have i ever seen such a huge spherical mass of glowing light, a translucent space of continuum that seems to enclose a holy celestial realm of gleaming light in glades and lustre of miniature stars and constellas ..

have i ever seen a such a elusive space that possesses a luminance so sacred with shdes of milder yellow sheen and lambent gleams so queer and quail it seems inside, such a cynosure of glowing irradiance it holds encore so bright in intense flames of such majesty .. so serene and so quintessential it seems inside ..

bounded by a layer of glass like translucent wall that is so subtle and thin in the midst of this circumferential dark ambien, while hovering alone in a lonely plane of terrain sans gravity sans any other breathing entity around, in this prevailing holy silence. Have i ever seen such a huge spherical mass of glowing light ..

I am your light ..
I am within you ..
and you re within me ..

says a gentle voice so true and so pure out of the glowing cynosure ..

the voice that seems to hold the answer that he is desperately in need of, the voice that seems to possess his innate understanding his yearn and his longing, that could heal and cure, that could revive and converge him onto his uno light of utmost prominance, the light that could resusciate him to life away from darkness, that could even enlighten him to a levitating hover, the light that could raise him to the higher refulgence of awakening and perhaps might even transcend beyond.

I am your light ..
I am within you ..
and you re within me ..
says a gentle voice so true and so pure out of the glowing cynosure ..

29
the seeker ..

the seeker ..

how long do you think the way of a seeker is ..

the journey might be too far say apart a seven hills,

seas and lands as you would read in mythical tales

rather it could even fall short of a couple of months time

say quite a distance in timeline ..

so deeper are his contemplations

with such a solid notion inside

the concerned contextual dwelling

to converge the elements rather the conceptions behind,

upon the innate slate of an individual

to perceive the reflections inside

in its relevant intensity rather the magnitude

of the light that you would throw

on the pertaining thread of an idea

while musing over a context's need or

the necessitated inside demand

surrounding the thread of a muse ..

the destination a seeker is afar from

that he is yearning to reach

the sort of innate desire that is binding

him toward the constant urge

 in looking out for his objective,

the urge that is gentle yet stern

in moving the seeker in his peregrination

in attaining his aim, the antidote, rather the panacea

for the lag owing to the distance of separation

that he has to traverse, that he has to go through,

overcome, rather he has to learn to raise himself

in gathering the relevant understanding or the exposures

that unravels him to the light,

perhaps rather the inner light,

the effulgence and beyond ..

what the seeker is seeking rather

his objective or the goal he has to attain,

the light and its radiance the seeker has to awaken himself with

entails persistence beneath the journey and the road

in converging the necessitated elements behind

the yearn that he has to satiate,

enduring the road, pain and the time

over the journey that might even be harsh

and obscure in its traverse,

at times might even be vague and dark

diverting you to a maze and oblivion,

despite the prevailing notion that

there is always this constant

proclivity inside this whole of nexus

toward him for what he is seeking

though the mystery surrounding this

unknown nexus fibre that begets this subtle link

is still not known to many and

remains quite difficult to perceive and obscure.

how long do you think the way of a seeker is ..

the journey might be too far say apart a seven hills,

seas and lands as you would read in mythical tales

rather it could even fall short of a couple of months time

say quite a distance in timeline ..

melancholy of a mystique medley dream .. & other selected poetry

30
the réfléchir ..

the réfléchir

an iota of sapien in the myriad matix

of infinite galaxies ..

 in deeper contemplations, would someone like to breathe ..

someone who would hover in an inebriative

space of a quaint queer trance ..

someone, inclined toward dwelling in the incessant

light of inner effulgence ..

seeking an awakening of the mind's convergence

toward the uno spot of deeper sensations

that might prevail pre lavitation ..

perhaps might even think about a neo enligtenment

that sort of a notch to an inch more

to the least post nirvana ..

in the depth of an ocean's musé ..

melancholy of a mystique medley dream .. & other selected poetry

31
the persistent latent
light ..

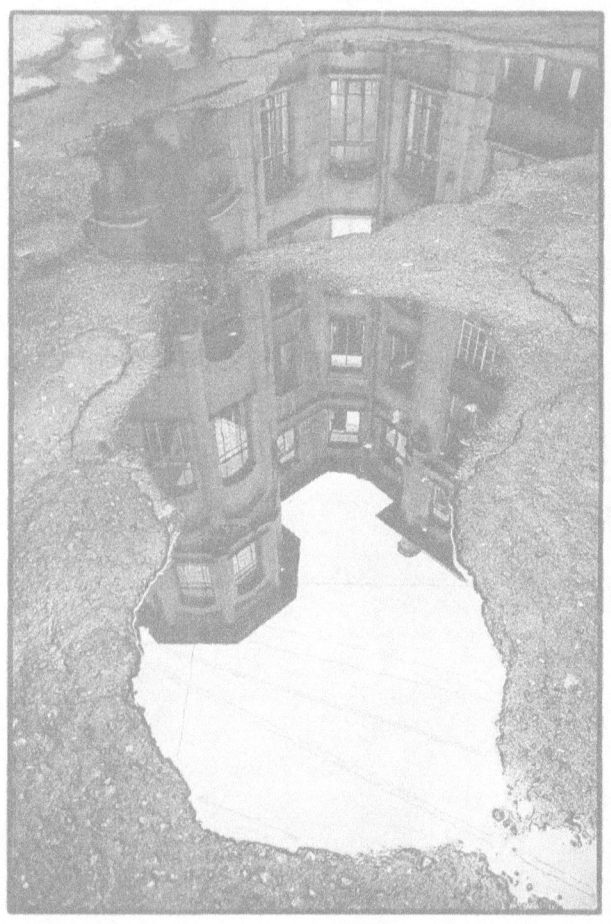

the persistent latent light ..

Seems a photographer's artistic capture of the ambien

in an unusual oblique angle through the waters' reflection.

Perhaps he might have tried to portray the sort of plight prevailing

in a milder grey tone over the waters and the kind of cracks and crevices

with the roughened texture might even be a tone to the beholder's mood

wherein he tries to picture the surrounding's scenario

in a vague frame of reflection projecting us the plight around

through the eerie windows, glasses and the inverted building

texturing the story behind its decades of stand though time,

witnessing its acquaintances, people who have inhabited the space

for years under its shelter dwelling in its shade,

while looking past their days of growth, progress, days of happiness,

times of grief, moments of love, lustre and life.

It has been seeing people grow, develop, their days of drive forward

through time, even might screen in slow frames of the resident's passage

over the ticking clock in a way to reminisce their lives

while throwing a light on the glimpse and gist of this

invertedly posing structure's traverse all along.

It's the light's incidence upon the surface of the rain waters,

reflecting us the building's pose in the layer of the waters

in those pits over the older roughened layer of ground's

darker side and earthiness lacking its appropriate demeanour,

captures this piece of artistic poster through the shutters and aperture

of the lens taking in the packets of photons and the patterns of lumen

via the beholder eyes' entailed substance rather by his artistic sense of gathering his thoughts, subtle ideas behind and the way he want

to articulate the frame's portraiture.

Its all about capturing the lumens of energy

into your gadget, converging them into

your prominent lens of the naked eye's luminance,

while taking it coherently inside for a certain aperture of the pupil,

necessitated over the shot for its iris iridescent outlay,

consequently gathering the incident patterns of lumen for

a certain amount of exposure before the shutter closes

assuming the intensity of incident rays to a germane candela,

depicting onto a engraved art form of a stolidly carved

scripture ode's substance extricating to the black

and white poster's milder surreal glade,

leading to portray its delinquent tinge behind

in a darker shade's aberrancy,

while exhuming fluent tones of striking grey hues

engrossed from the scene's inherent plight,

or the inlaid texture of quite a loss and

the persisting latent light.

32
i am all yours, oh my dear !!

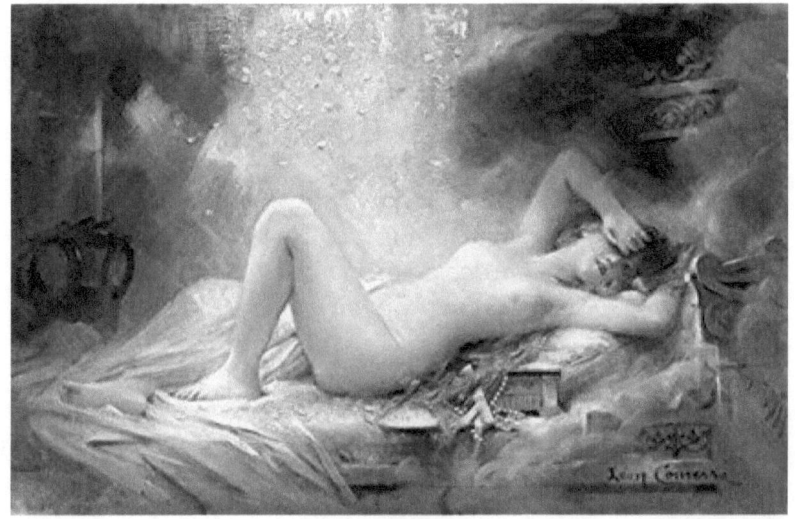

i am all yours, oh my dear !!

she is lying here in front me so beautiful and her naked flawless body so gleamingly glowing out of the shimmring pearl yellow light, thats lit low to set the darker space mood in the arousing milder hues upon the place that we are about to tryst on embarking a erotic peregrination over the sensual world far off, to gloom up the the present continuum as if its holding on a potioned blend of the sexual greek god's aura that would induce even a layman to the sublime seductions of the aphrodite's arousing.

i am just standing in here all lost in her exquisite pulchritude, utterly fallen by her femme fatale nudity. so charming is she urging me onto a inebriated poetical muse to croon on a lovely woo of the sexual greek god's romantic ballad, and so wilder is her womanhood curves that would seduce me on to the higher pleasures of erotica angels' sex haven.

she is in front of me all naked as the greek goddess' erotic light illuminating the space around that tends to ignite every last speck of lumen in the radiance to a seductress fire of lascivious desires, that seems to migrate alive the iridescent portraits of the greek god's painted love scenes' regal intimacy, and even that divine light perhaps could be possessing the eternal blaze of the glorious holy twine flame, which indeed is the root of the erotica fire's enigmatic beatitude toward the higher desires of lewd and love.

oh there, she is all nude lying there in front of me, as if she sings

' i am all yours now, for you to awe, for you to revel about in your sexy reverie, for you to lyric on my beauty and womanhood, for you to paint my glow in a stupendous naked portrait, for you to muse about my arousing features, to read over my body's eloquent curves, the elixir breasts, the undulating dark long hairs, the arousing back of lustre slide, getting down to my heavenly groove inviting your manhood to intimate together and the every last inch of this elegant sculpt of sex godess, to the everything upon me as me.

i am all in here lying naked in front of you, oh dear, so you would come over and revel inside of me so that you would intertwine with my body glowing in the blaze of the holy twine flame with all relishing pleasures of the erotica sex angels, so that we would dwell as one, as us, reviving every expression of the sexual greek god's intricate postures and forms that relams the aphrodite parchment depicting pictoral intimacies, to deeply contemplate our orgasms triggered by the exalted greek gods and godesses of the myriad erotica angels culminated together, elevating ourselves over the immortal sexual trance of love, lust and romance.

i am all yours here, oh my dear man, so come and revel inside of me '

33
i am all yours, oh my dear
.. part ii

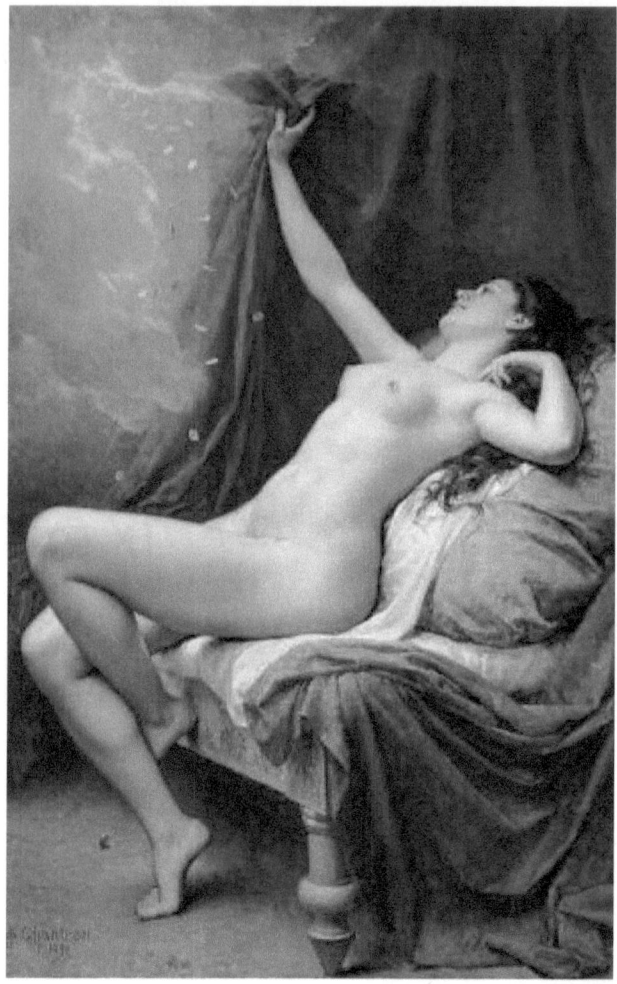

i am all yours, oh my dear .. part ii

' oh my mighty adonis, i am all yours oh dear, come feel my scent of sensual youth's exhilarating womanhood, the soothing redolent of mine which might have originated from the petals of the erotica land's lovely blooms taking you high through to the odour of sexual heaven, turning you on seducing the insides of you like the congression of lord kama's seductions would coagulate to streamline the tiny molecules in the continumm that posesses the hazy blend inducing the stoned sensations of the cute little scarletts blossomed from the erotica angels' sex flora, inching your insides with the intertwining twists and turns of firing desires that has flamed out of its eerie prolonging fizz onto its sinful seductions.

oh dear, the perfume of mine might elevate you to the hypnotized states that would prevail inside the land of sexual inebriation's apogee, right from your nasal conduit till its reach over to the brain's sensing space making you feel my sincintilating womanhood's blissful fragrance and the ardent love of my fountain youth's salascious springs. the seducing scent of mine my dear, would pull you to my arena of love hypnosis, inducing your inner sex whirls wildly while profligating the continuum's molecule sieze by the sex scent's inherent miniature aural blaze that aint no visible to our pupil's retinal sense, coalescing them to our rendevouz's innate exuberance of incessant sex, romance and ecstatic love.

oh my man, the odour of my enthralling naked beauty might even aloft you to the sensations of the erotica land's greek god erection, that would take us to the orgasms of the mighty sex gods, while we are in a cease less intercourse of days together witnessing every dawn's raise, the dusk's gloom, and the kissing moonlight's radiance of deeper intimacies and passionate love.

oh my dear man, its the fragrance of love calling unto you, to revel inside of me to drink my wine of fountain youth, to dwell in my exotic intimacy and to derive pleasures through the exploring desires of the highness lord kama's lassitude. its the scent you love, you adore and shell yourself with, its the holy fragrance of erotica sex angles' enormous culmination that you yearn to adorn, the perfume of the love potion's seducing concoction immersing us onto the perennial pleasures of lust, sex and everlasting love.

and oh the odour of love,
the scent of heaven,
the scent of my love,
is all around us in this sensual continuum we acquiesce,

let you smell its rejuvenating air of bliss, let you feel its exfoliating
sense of heaven's drizzle ..

let you muse about
its deeper penetrating
invisible murky aura's
love hypnosis
with your lady aegis,
let you trance and adorn
its serene sheath
of my love ..

let you hear its
erotica call
of lewd arousal,
to intertwine in this
rendezvous of
intimate aria,
to intercourse in
this tryst of sex,

to revel inside of me,
oh my dear ..

34
i am all yours, oh my dear
.. part iii

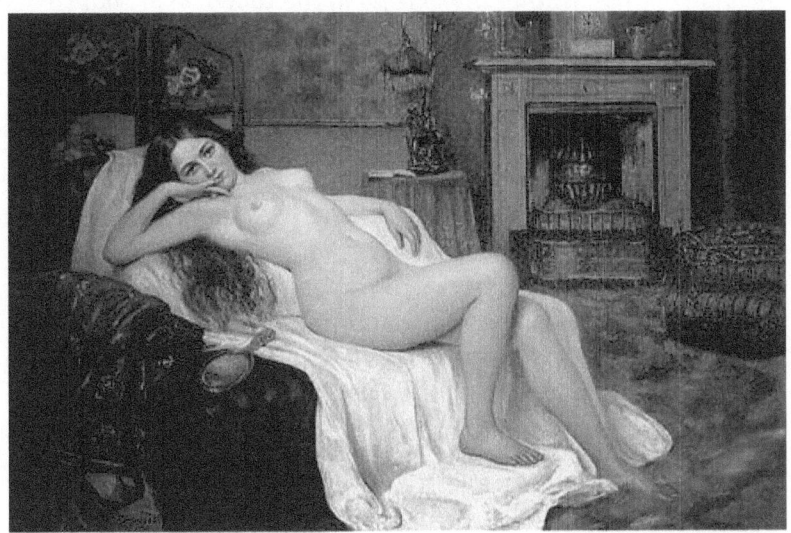

i am all yours, oh my dear .. part i ii

Oh my dear man, i am all naked in this sensual space of ours, for you to relish my womanhood and embellish our times of fervid passion inside this trysting continuum of ours.

I am lying in here lasciviously nude, for you oh my dear,

for you to sensually get into me while you gently push my intimate part toward your manhood brushing my erotic butts. Sliding your hands, that is electrifying the touch on my naked impeccable body, through my pale soft skin of golden lustre back slide as you try to seduce me, like the lords of erotica angels fill in the seductor potion of salacious springs upon the desperate muggles or the materialistic mud bloods in their delusional continuum of mind's inner core to ablaze them with the firing desires of passionate togetherness from the twine flame, to redirect them with libido of intricate sex manoeuvres longing for passionate intimacy's apogee. I am all yours for your naked male body to brush against my female voluptuous womanhood's loving bosoms, which would raise up the ardent passion of lewd and love, turning us wilder in the lewdland of the aphrodites, to drink the lustful wines of arousing substances intoxicating us to the sense of lewdland's intimate aria.

Oh my dear, i am in here, for you to hold me in your arms,

with us brushing against each other, with our sensual eyes connecting our inner souls while tying it together with the eternal love knot of intimate bonding and blazing desires of sexual indulgence, while you subtly whisper in my ears the cantos from deeply felt songs of unparalleled love, longing and yearn over my beauty and sex, while you romantically croon in your libretto from the erotica love songs of awe, encomiums and engrossed eulogy exalting my beauty and infallible womanhood. Together we muse the poetry of your love, erotica and embracing eulogy, revelling in its engrossing emotions that raises the firing desires of overwhelming romance ablaze and pleasures behind literary allusions and awe, intaking its drinks of inebriating sexual potion steaming our passions and mood higher.

Oh my man i am all yours, for you to embrace me,

for you to slow kiss my ear lobes, for you to sensually kiss my rosy cheeks as if your upper and lower lip tries to sexily moonwalk toward my lips down from the lobes exhuming the incandescent aura of lustful times that prevails in the lewdland of aphrodites while they intercourse, which seems to have stemmed up from the fragrance of the lewdland's laevender which has a significant variation on juxtaposing with its muggle counterpart owing to its inherent sex gloss.

You deeply kiss my intoxicating lips

that oozes out the aging wines

while dipping down dews of honey,

with the passions of the frenchmen intimacy,

so milder and so wilder,

so deeper and so engrossed,

as you bite it mildly

you try to suck it wildly,

as you chew it sensually

you drink its wine lustfully,

as you suck it again to

taste its libidinous honey,

just when it exults us to the

lewdland's ecstatic sex whirls;

as our tongues play

with each other

you try to suck mine,

when we intertwine

 as our linging buds

interchanges saliva,

and our clinging kiss

seems to

cease never;

while i close my eyes

feeling the acme of passion

that is taking us high

to the notch of stoned times

from the aging juices of

the frenchmen vineyard,

to the lewdland's

kissing hay of

wilder exuberance;

i am all yours naked and ripe, oh my man,

for you to kiss my neck, lick my nape, as you write songs of lust and lyrics of love around it for hours and hours together over the region and below as you lick, kiss and brush your inner lip moistening the skin around over and over while our times of sensual indulgence gets the right trigger. You get down seated on our sex bed kissing my navel licking its hole gently, as I cafuné your hairs with milder moans of scintillating pleasures arousing each other while you feel the exquisite aria of sensual fondness from your beloved's slow moaning with her eyes closed, as in the tunes of mozart's and vivaldi's orchestration to the romantic ballads. Just as you kiss my navel you caress my breasts intimately with a hand while holding me with another, you slowly manoeuvre to my hip in my flaming body, you kiss, you lick, you suck and linger around, over and over around my abdomen and navel before getting over to my bosoms, while i groan and moan mildly continuing my tunes of wilder pleasures and endearing romantic bliss.

35
i am all yours, oh my
dear .. part iv

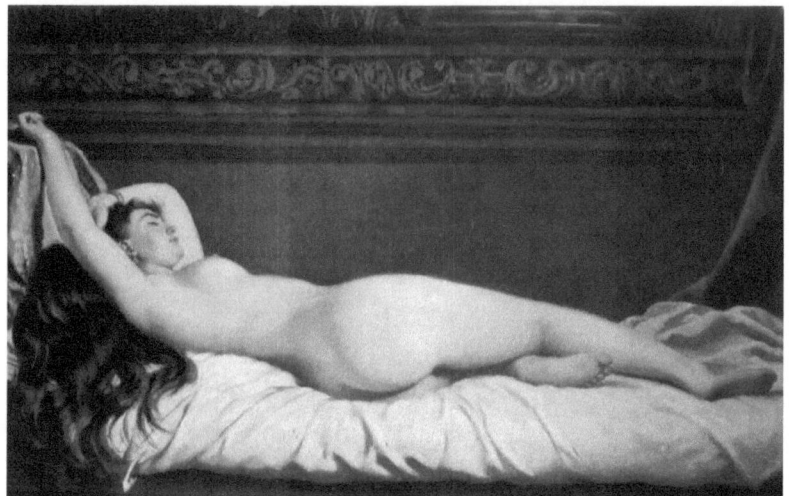

i am all yours, oh my dear .. part iv

you kiss and caress my lovely breasts affectionately feeling its warmth and revelling in its delicate womanhood of the aphrodite's beauty. You fondly kiss my firm and supple breasts of the feminine beauty's eloquent curves, you lick and suck my nipples, you linger around my areola as my nipples gets mildly aroused to its firmness, you plant your lips over my cleavage and kiss it around and toward my neck sensually, as we revel in sexual joy of the lewdland angels' overture pleasures, you suck my nipples gently that is oozing out the lactating white milk of nourishing love and flourishing sweetness, while you drink it enjoying our mating feed, pleasuring me to the ecstasy of lewdland sex whirls as you quench you thirst of sex and womanhood's scintillating intimacy, as we are sensually engaged in passionate love of sex's overture and intimately engrossed in its exquisite sexual carousing.

You innately muse over

my beautiful womanhood

curves kissing and caressing it,

feeling the sensual indulgence's

aura flaming our passions

so endearing and so closer,

while bringing alive

the play of overture

migrating it from the

lewdland aphrodite and

greek god intercourse,

so fervently with glowing

amour of the lovestruck cupids,

so passionately with the scintillating

womanhood's adorning embrace,

so intimately amidst

the lady aegis embossed

by her heavenly curves

and the mighty adonis'

armour of zeal,

as in the lewdland

flux of sex creating around

a sheath of lovely intimate aria

embracing them by the chill breeze's

orchestrated sonnet of bliss,

dwelling inside the intertwined bonding

of pure love and sizzling romance.

I am all yours oh my dear, inside this magnificent rotunda, our tryst of love, our rendezvous of sex,

You kiss my lips so lovingly over the slow sliding waters on my face, while you glide your hands around my seducing back's lustre and pushing in my vagina toward your manhood feeling my butt as you mildly try to press and squeeze it.

we continue kissing and

holding each other so close and so sensually,

wetting ourselves in those

milder lucid streams of the sex rivulet,

that is seducing us so intimately

glistening us with

the aphrodite's arousing,

making us feel the wilder seducing

current of the fire and ice

in a delusional paradigm

yet certainly felt in real,

divulging us to the resplendent

freezing ablaze,

the flames of the twine,

the fire of love,

instilling us the sex whirls of the

early virgin erotica angels and

exfoliating us with the desires of

the aphrodite's sex cantata,

streaming us the lewdland lovers'

ravishing slender showers of

the heaven's rain and

their serene drizzle of the lascivious springs,

taking us along toward the

salascious flames of the freezing sex streams'

eloquent indulgence,

exulting the two of us to pleasures

of scintillating cupid streams,

as we stand intertwined as uno

alongside the deeply felt inner

desires of lust and love,

showering the rain of heaven and

pouring the serene drizzle of love

augmented by the filling of sexual unction

shimmering our inner longing and lustre,

while migrating us to

a tryst of a libidinous muse.

as we get down lustfully

into the tub of sex fluids

that possesses the diluted love potion's

aura of sinful seductions,

inducing us the wilder erotica pleasures

of cupid streams and sex angels

of the lady waters, culminated together

immersing our insides with

the aphrodite arousal so unique

of this tub fluids and

the reclining lovers' graceful play,

so soothingly arousing us to the

lewdland lady nile's colossal

spread of love, care,

warmth and passionate intimacies.

we immerse ourselves in this tub

of sex lactations so pure and

so white possessing the seductor

potion of the cupid's sex secretions,

wherein it is floating

the myriad sex scintillas

of mirth and glow.

We are soaked in the tub of love,

immersed in its embrace of warm

seductions we revel in

its lascivious lactations.

i turn toward your face sliding my hands

through your hairs as i kiss your lips

intimately and seduce you

with sex lavender intricacies and

the glow of the erotica angels.

I sensually kiss, lick and caress your cheeks,

neck and the adonis' mighty arms

while you lovingly engage in

our soothing pleasures of lewd and love

with your lady aegis.

We continue our tryst in this

tub of cupid streams,

feeling the dip of a quenching hay,

we are immersed in a libidinous muse,

we are deeply engaged in

a lovely sensual indulgence,

transcending ourselves to a incessant

flow of the intimate aria,

radiating the mating flames around us

to a sexual illuminance of lust and light,

to a sensual fire of gleam and glow,

to the existing aura's quintessential love

and pure romantic bliss.

acknowledgements

*i would like to thank all the women who ve been my inspiration ,
whom i v e admired and adored, who have helped me in writing
my poems, say a stranger from a random magazine photograph
or someone whom i know, may be a friend or an ex, who have
been around me and who have knowingly or unknowingly urged
me in my writing and muse, may be a random girl you pass by in
a mall or a nude museum painting, it could be a tiny spark inside
your senses to a daydream, or a lasting impression inside you
through its charm, art and beauty, pushing you to admire,
dream, muse , lyricize and write. I should thank each and every
one of them for inspiring me and being a part in my writing and
poetry, may be a quick glance, rather a short span's gaze or a
painting in my wall years together.*

*also i thank all my friends, folks and peers who ve been around
me and who have helped me in shaping muself the way i am
now, through their guide and support..*

about the author

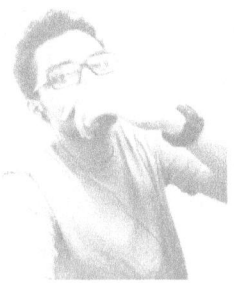

prasad hirsch

author is a mechanical engineer working with a middle east petrochem construction firm, who writes and blogs on his random thoughts, ideas and certain other interests. A passionate artiste who draws his inspiration from nature, beauty and art, likes to sketch portraits every other weekend (his art gallery fb.me/strokenshade) and has such love for photography too. Being a fitness enthusiast, has a firm leaning toward meditation. spends his leisure time reading, watching movies and singing his favourite unplugged tunes.

you could reach him @hariprasad.mails1@gmail.com

melancholy of a mystique medley dream .. & other selected poetry

www.ingramcontent.com/pod-product-compliance
Lightning Source LLC
Chambersburg PA
CBHW030620220526
45463CB00004B/1362